Blooming Bouquet Album

Dena's Tip

Paint tulips down the center of a 10 1/4" length of ribbon for a bookmark to give to an avid reader.

Gather It:

- 13" square canvas photo album
- 2" wide striped grosgrain ribbon
- Liquitex® Soft Body Professional Artist Colors: Cadmium Yellow Light Hue, Sap Green Permanent, Medium Magenta, Titanium White, Light Green Permanent, Naphthol Crimson, Cadmium Red Light, Light Violet, and Light Blue Permanent
- Liquitex® Fabric Medium
- #2 round paintbrush
- Ranger Stickles™ glitter glue: Golden Rod
- General supplies: tracing paper, transfer paper, a palette, a container of water, and paper towels
- Fabric glue

Paint It:

Add one part Fabric Medium to each of the colors and color mixtures used to paint the album. Rinse and blot the paintbrush on a paper towel between each color. Let the paint dry after each application.

1. Cut a length of ribbon 2" longer than the front of the album.
2. Paint the tulip stems and leaves on the ribbon with Cadmium Yellow Light Hue + Sap Green Permanent. (Practice on a scrap piece of ribbon to make sure that the paint mixture isn't too watery and that it doesn't bleed through the ribbon.)
3. Paint the tulips with Medium Magenta + Titanium White.
4. Highlight the leaves with Light Green Permanent. Add a touch of Naphthol Crimson to the tulips.
5. Trace, then transfer the bouquet pattern from the pattern insert onto the album.
6. Paint the flower centers with Cadmium Yellow Light Hue + Cadmium Red Light. Dot around the bouquet with this color also.

Meet Dena Fishbein

"Embellish your life" is Dena Fishbein's motto. Dena is the host of her own hit television show, "Embellish This!" on the DIY Network. She is also the creative director of Dena Designs, Inc., producing dinnerware, giftware, infant and juvenile bedding, stationery, fabrics, and home accessories.

Dena Designs began as a notebook of sketches that flourished into a successful company after Dena showed her work to a licensing agent. And while Dena is an artist first and foremost, her involvement with her company is hands-on; she regularly works with her clients to enhance their products with her playfully chic designs. Dena has also developed a publishing program. She writes a monthly syndicated newspaper column on design and is the winner of 17 Louie Awards (for greeting card designs), as well as the Greeting Card of the Year award.

Like many artists, Dena didn't originally plan on a career in product design. After graduating from UCLA with a degree in landscape architecture and industrial design, she moved to New York City. A newspaper advertisement led to a job with an agency that sold art to textile manufacturers. Soon a Dena-designed bedding collection was on the cover of a Bloomingdale's catalog, and Dena became recognized for the fresh, uncontrived fabric designs that set her work apart.

Dena now lives and works in sunny California with her husband, Danny, and their three children. As a mother, Dena knows there are just so many hours in every woman's day, which is why she encourages women to take a relaxed, happy approach to decorating. In return, Dena has won a huge following and has been labeled "a lifestyle embellisher extraordinaire."

"I love to embellish," says Dena, "because you don't have to start from scratch. You can easily and inexpensively add your own personal style to everything, from your wardrobe to your home. Embellishing is for everyone, from children to adults of every age. It is especially great for those of us (like me!) who are intimidated by big, daunting projects. And it's perfect for those of us who just want to have fun in the process."

Pampered Pet Bowls

Dena's Tip

Dots are easy to paint using the end of a paintbrush or a stylus. Simply dip the end of the brush or stylus into paint and then touch the end to the project.

Gather It:

- Pastel ceramic bowls
- Liquitex® Glossies™ high-gloss acrylic enamel paints: Pink, Yellow, White, Green, and Red
- #2 round paintbrush
- General supplies: a palette, a container of water, and paper towels

Paint It:

Rinse and blot the paintbrush on a paper towel between each color. Let the paint dry after each application.

1. Paint Pink stripes every 2" around the bowl.
2. Paint a Yellow stripe on each side of the Pink stripes.
3. Mix Pink and White together and paint dots between each set of stripes for the rosebuds.
4. Mix Yellow and Green together on the palette and paint the leaves between the rosebuds.
5. Add a touch of Red to the bottom of each rosebud and a touch of Green to the bottom of each leaf.

7. Paint the flower petals with Medium Magenta + Titanium White, Light Violet, Medium Magenta, or Cadmium Red Light.
8. Paint the stems and leaves with Cadmium Yellow Light Hue + Sap Green Permanent. Dot the spine of the album with this color also.
9. Highlight the leaves with Light Green Permanent, then Light Blue Permanent.
10. Outline the bow with Light Violet and the bouquet flowers and leaves with glitter as desired.
11. Glue the ribbon to the side of the album, wrapping the ends to the inside.

Chic Chair Cover

Dena's Tip

Paint the three-stroke designs with "comma" strokes. Place the tip of the paintbrush at the top of each stroke, apply slight pressure to the bristles of the brush while pulling down and then release the pressure on the bristles, rolling the brush tip back to a point.

Gather It:

- Off-white canvas chair cover for a Parson's chair
- Liquitex® Soft Body Professional Artist Color: Ivory Black
- Liquitex® Fabric Medium
- #2 round paintbrush
- General supplies: tracing paper, transfer paper, a palette, a container of water, and paper towels

Paint It:

Add one part Fabric Medium to the paint. Rinse and blot the paintbrush on a paper towel between each color. Let the paint dry after each application.

1. Use a pencil and ruler to draw evenly spaced diagonal lines across the seat of the chair cover. (The lines on our chair cover are approximately 1 1/2" apart.)
2. Outline the diagonal lines and paint a three-stroke design at the center of each of the diamonds with Ivory Black (see Dena's Tip for help painting the designs).
3. Trace, then transfer the border pattern from the pattern insert onto the skirt of the chair cover. Or, if you prefer, freehand the pattern onto the skirt. Also, freehand a swirl border around the top of the chair cover.
4. Outline the border lines with Ivory Black.

Flowerific Frame

Dena's Tip

Use masking tape to hold the wooden shapes steady while you are painting. All you have to do is place a length of masking tape, sticky side up, on your work surface. Now, stick the wooden shapes onto the tape, paint, and peel off of the tape when the paint is dry.

Gather It:

- 5" x 7" wooden frame with routed edges
- Eight 1/2" wooden tulips
- Eight 1/2" wooden flowers
- Matte white spray paint
- Liquitex® Soft Body Professional Artist Colors: Medium Magenta, Titanium White, Cadmium Red Light, Cadmium Yellow Light Hue, and Sap Green Permanent
- Liner, #1 round, and 1/2" flat paintbrushes
- General supplies: a palette, a container of water, and paper towels
- Wood glue

Paint It:

Rinse and blot the paintbrush on a paper towel between each color. Let the paint dry after each application. Use spray paint in a well-ventilated area.

1. Spray paint the frame, tulips, and flowers.
2. Paint the tulips with Medium Magenta + Titanium White. Use the liner to outline the tops of the tulips with Cadmium Red Light.
3. Paint the flowers with Cadmium Red Light + Cadmium Yellow Light Hue. Dot the flower centers with Cadmium Yellow Light Hue.
4. Arrange and glue the tulips and flowers on the frame.
5. Use the #1 round brush to paint the stems and leaves with Sap Green Permanent + Cadmium Yellow Light Hue.
6. Use the 1/2" flat brush to paint Medium Magenta + Titanium White stripes along the edge of the frame.

Appealing Pots

Dena's Tip

If these pots are exposed to water they will rust over time. Be sure to place potted plants with saucers in your pots and hide the top of the pots with moss, vines, or greenery.

Gather It:

- Galvanized metal pots
- DecoArt™ No-Prep Metal Paint™: Coal Black, Bright Lime Green, Hunter Green, Lagoon Blue, Bright Yellow, Real Red, and Strawberry Shake
- #2 round paintbrush
- General painting supplies: vinegar, tracing paper, transfer paper, a palette, a container of water, and paper towels

Paint It:

Rinse and blot the paintbrush on a paper towel between each color. Let the paint dry after each application.

1. Clean the pot with vinegar. Rinse the pot with water and allow to dry thoroughly.
2. Trace, then transfer the desired flower pattern from page 30 onto the front of the pot. Also transfer or freehand the border pattern around the top of the pot.
3. Paint the flowerpot and the border with Coal Black.
4. Paint the stems and leaves with Bright Lime Green. Shade the stems and leaves with Hunter Green + Bright Lime Green.
5. Paint the blue flowers with Lagoon Blue.
6. Paint the yellow flowers with Bright Yellow. Paint the flower centers with Real Red.
7. Paint the pink flowers with Strawberry Shake. Dot the flower centers with Real Red.

Cheery Glass Plate

Dena's Tip

Paint the cherries with large dots and "C" strokes. First, swirl the paint around to create a large dot. Now, paint a "C" on one side of the dot, leaving an unpainted area in the center of the cherry for the highlight. It's that simple!

Gather It:

- 8" diameter glass plate
- FolkArt® Enamels™: Medium Magenta, Autumn Leaves, Hauser Green Medium, Lemon Custard, Baby Pink, and Frost Medium
- #4 round paintbrush
- General supplies: tracing paper, removable tape, a palette, a container of water, and paper towels

Paint It:

Rinse and blot the paintbrush on a paper towel between each color. Let the paint dry after each application.

1. Trace the pattern from page 30 onto tracing paper; cut the pattern out. Trace over the pattern lines on the back side of the pattern. Tape the pattern, right side up, to the top of the plate. Turn the plate over and, moving the pattern as necessary, paint the design on the back side of the plate.
2. Paint the wavy line around the edge of the plate with Medium Magenta and Autumn Leaves.
3. Paint cherry bunches around the plate with Medium Magenta, leaving approximately 2" between the bunches (see Dena's Tip for help painting the cherries). After the paint is dry, add a second coat of paint to make the cherries more opaque.
4. Paint the leaves, stems, and wavy lines between the cherry bunches with Hauser Green Medium + Lemon Custard.
5. Outline one side of each leaf with Hauser Green Medium. Outline one side of each cherry with Baby Pink.
6. Dot between the cherry bunches with Frost Medium.

Charming Tote Bag

Dena's Tip

Place a short length of tape across the pom-pom trim before you cut it and then cut through the center of the tape. This keeps the ends from raveling.

Gather It:

- Large canvas tote
- Liquitex® Soft Body Professional Artist Colors: Medium Magenta, Titanium White, Cadmium Yellow Light Hue, Sap Green Permanent, Light Blue Permanent, Cadmium Red Light, and Light Violet
- Liquitex® Fabric Medium
- #3 round and 1/2" and 1" flat paintbrushes
- General supplies: tracing paper, transfer paper, a palette, a container of water, and paper towels
- 1" diameter green flower button
- 1/2" diameter blue button
- Pink pom-pom trim
- Fabric glue

Paint It:

Add one part Fabric Medium to each of the colors and color mixtures used to paint the bag. Rinse and blot the paintbrush on a paper towel between each color. Let the paint dry after each application.

1. Use the 1" flat brush to paint the band at the top of the tote with Medium Magenta + Titanium White. Use the 1/2" flat brush to paint the stripes on the handles with the same color.
2. Trace, then transfer the heart pattern from the pattern insert onto the front of the tote bag and the flower border pattern onto the band at the top. Freehand the borders at the top and bottom of the tote bag.
3. Paint the green stems and leaves with Cadmium Yellow Light Hue + Sap Green Permanent. Shade the leaves with a touch of Sap Green Permanent.
4. Use the #3 round brush to paint the blue leaves with Light Blue Permanent.
5. Use the #3 round brush to paint the pink flowers with Medium Magenta + Titanium White. Dot the flower centers with Cadmium Red Light.

6. Paint the purple flower petals with Light Violet. Dot the flower centers with Cadmium Yellow Light Hue.
7. Paint the white flowers with Titanium White. Dot the flower centers with Cadmium Red Light.
8. Paint the border at the top of the tote bag with Cadmium Yellow Light Hue + Sap Green Permanent. Paint, then dot the border at the bottom of the bag with Medium Magenta + Titanium White.
9. Layer and sew the buttons on the band at the top of the bag. Glue a length of pom-pom trim across the bottom of the bag.

Petaled Placemat Set

Dena's Tip

Don't skip painting this project because an orange napkin doesn't match your kitchen décor. Just buy napkins and placemats in your favorite color and adjust the shading color on the petals to coordinate with them.

Gather It:

- Orange cloth napkin
- Coordinating cloth placemat
- Liquitex® Soft Body Professional Artist Colors: Titanium White, Medium Magenta, Cadmium Yellow Light Hue, Sap Green Permanent, and Naphthol Crimson
- Liquitex® Fabric Medium
- #2 round paintbrush
- General supplies: tracing paper, transfer paper, a palette, a container of water, and paper towels

Paint It:

Add one part Fabric Medium to each of the colors and color mixtures used to paint the napkin and placemat. Rinse and blot the paintbrush on a paper towel between each color. Let the paint dry after each application.

1. Trace, then transfer the flower pattern from page 29 onto the napkin and the border pattern onto the napkin and placemat.
2. Paint the flower and borders with two coats of Titanium White.
3. Shade the tip of each flower petal with Medium Magenta + Titanium White.
4. Shade the base of each leaf, dot above the leaves on the flower, and outline the stem with Cadmium Light Yellow Hue + Sap Green Permanent. Add a touch of the same color to the dots at the flower center.
5. Shade around the dots at the flower center with Naphthol Crimson.

Hydrangea Pillow

Dena's Tip

Remove the pillow form from the pillow cover before you paint. Slide a piece of cardboard inside the pillow cover to prevent the paint from bleeding through to the other side.

Gather It:

- 20" square decorator pillow with a green cover
- Liquitex® Soft Body Professional Artist Colors: Light Violet, Medium Magenta, Light Blue Violet, Titanium White, Sap Green Permanent, Cadmium Yellow Light Hue, Olive, Permanent Bleu Clair, Phthalocyanine Blue, and Cadmium Red Light
- Liquitex® Fabric Medium
- #4 round paintbrush
- General supplies: tracing paper, transfer paper, a palette, a container of water, and paper towels

Paint It:

Add one part Fabric Medium to each of the colors and color mixtures used to paint the pillow. Rinse and blot the paintbrush on a paper towel between each color. Let the paint dry after each application.

1. Trace, then transfer the flower and border patterns from the pattern insert onto the pillow.
2. Paint the heart-shaped hydrangea petals with Light Violet + Medium Magenta + Light Blue Violet. Make each hydrangea blossom loose but slightly rounded.
3. Add Light Blue Violet and Light Blue Violet + Titanium White on the hydrangea petals as shading or loose outlines.
4. Paint the stems and leaves with Sap Green Permanent + Cadmium Yellow Light Hue + Titanium White. Shade the leaves with Olive.
5. Paint the blue flower petals with Light Blue Violet + Titanium White + Permanent Bleu Clair. Shade the blue flower petals with Phthalocyanine Blue.
6. Paint the rosebuds with Titanium White + Medium Magenta. Shade the rosebuds with Cadmium Red Light.
7. Highlight the leaves, blue flowers, and rosebuds and dot the hydrangea centers with Titanium White.

Refreshing Watering Can

Dena's Tip

Topcoat the watering can with No-Prep Metal Paint Clear Medium to "seal" and protect your painting from outdoor elements.

Gather It:

- Galvanized metal watering can
- DecoArt™ No-Prep Metal Paint™: Bright White, Strawberry Shake, Real Red, Bright Yellow, Bright Lime Green, and Hunter Green
- #4 round paintbrush
- General supplies: vinegar, tracing paper, transfer paper, a palette, a container of water, and paper towels

Paint It:

Rinse and blot the paintbrush on a paper towel between each color. Let the paint dry after each application.

1. Clean the watering can with vinegar. Rinse the watering can with water and allow to dry thoroughly.
2. Trace, then transfer the flower pattern from the pattern insert onto the front of the watering can.
3. Pick up Bright White and Strawberry Shake on the brush and begin to paint the flower petals. Continue painting the petals, occasionally picking up Real Red on the brush in addition to the Bright White and Strawberry Shake.
4. Pick up Bright Yellow and Bright Lime Green on the brush and begin to paint the leaves. Continue painting the leaves, occasionally picking up Hunter Green on the brush in addition to the Bright Yellow and Bright Lime Green.
5. Paint the bow and the wavy borders at the top and bottom with Strawberry Shake.

Dainty Duvet & Sham Set

Dena's Tip

Follow the fabric medium manufacturer's instructions to heat set the painted designs with an iron. This will allow you to launder the duvet cover and pillow shams.

Gather It:

- White duvet cover
- White pillow shams
- Liquitex® Soft Body Professional Artist Colors: Cerulean Blue, Titanium White, Light Blue Permanent, Phthalocyanine Blue, Mars Black, and Cadmium Yellow Medium Hue
- Liquitex® Fabric Medium
- #5 and #6 round paintbrushes
- General supplies: tracing paper, transfer paper, containers for water and paints, and paper towels
- Coordinating lace trim

Paint It:

Do not rinse out the paintbrush between the colors used for this project. The key to this technique is to paint the flowers quickly. Let the paint dry after each application.

1. Trace, then transfer the pattern from page 28 onto the duvet cover and the edges of the pillow shams as desired.
2. Begin by adding the following colors or color mixes to the containers: Cerulean Blue + Titanium White, Light Blue Permanent, Phthalocyanine Blue + Titanium White, Phthalocyanine Blue + Mars Black + Titanium White, Light Blue Permanent + Cadmium Yellow Medium Hue, and Cadmium Yellow Medium Hue. Now, add fabric medium and a bit of water to each of the colors or color mixes.
3. Test the colors on a scrap piece of fabric to make sure that the paints aren't too watery and that they won't bleed. You may want to place a piece of cardboard inside the duvet cover or sham to prevent the paint from bleeding through to the other side.

4. Dip the brush into water and then into one of the lighter shades of blue paint. Now begin painting the four heart-shaped petals on one of the flowers. Keep the brush wet and use a very light and easy touch.
5. Continue painting the flowers, using all three of the lighter shades of blue paint. Don't wash out the brush between colors – dip the brush in one shade of blue and then into the next shade to make your flower petals more interesting.
6. Outline the flower petals as desired with the darkest shade of blue. Dot the flower centers with the Cadmium Yellow Medium Hue.
7. Paint the stems and leaves with the green paint color. When painting the stems, it is important to think about spacing. Try to space the stems at regular intervals.
8. After the paint is dry, sew the coordinating trim to the edges of the pillow sham openings.

Whimsical Frame Box

Dena's Tip

You don't always have to place photographs in frames. This box presents the perfect opportunity to showcase a favorite drawing or an image cut from a greeting card.

Gather It:

- $6^1/_2$" x $2^3/_4$" x $4^7/_8$" wooden photo box
- Four $^5/_8$" diameter wooden beads
- White spray primer
- Liquitex® Soft Body Professional Artist Colors: Light Blue Violet, Titanium White, Raw Sienna, Cadmium Yellow Light Hue, Sap Green Permanent, Phthalocyanine Blue, Bright Aqua Green, and Iridescent Gold Deep
- #1 liner and $^1/_2$" flat paintbrushes
- Krylon® 18 Kt. Gold Leafing Pen
- General supplies: a palette, a container of water, and paper towels
- Wood glue
- FolkArt® Finishes-Clearcote™ Aerosol Glaze – Hi-Shine Deep Gloss
- $^3/_4$" diameter cream button
- Jewel glue

Paint It:

Rinse and blot the paintbrush on a paper towel between each color. Let the paint dry after each application. Use spray primer and glaze in a well-ventilated area.

1. Spray the box and beads with primer.
2. Use the $^1/_2$" flat brush to paint the sides of the box and the blue border on top of the box with Light Blue Violet + Titanium White.
3. Use the #1 liner brush to paint the flowers and leaves on the blue areas with Titanium White + Raw Sienna as shown.
4. Shade the flowers with Light Blue Violet + water. Shade the leaves with Cadmium Yellow Light Hue + Sap Green Permanent. Dot the flower centers with Light Blue Violet.
5. Paint the grey-blue border around the frame opening and the latticework on the white border at the edge of the lid with Phthalocyanine Blue + Titanium White.
6. Paint the aqua borders with Bright Aqua Green + Titanium White + Phthalocyanine Blue.

7. Paint the leaves and stem on the bottom aqua border with Light Blue Violet. Dot the aqua and white borders at the edge of the lid with this color also.
8. Add details to the design with the gold leafing pen as shown. Paint the wooden beads with Iridescent Gold Deep.
9. Use wood glue to glue the beads to the bottom of the box for the "feet."
10. Apply two coats of glaze to the box.
11. Use jewel glue to glue the button to the box clasp.

Berries & Blooms Tray

Dena's Tip

Spattering is a great way to add character to painted items and it's simple to do. Just cover your work surface with newspaper, dip the bristles of an old toothbrush in thinned paint, and run your thumb over the bristles to flick the paint onto the surface.

Gather It:

- 13 1/4" x 10 1/4" wooden tray
- 1 1/4" wooden ball knobs
- White spray primer
- Liquitex® Soft Body Professional Artist Colors: Light Blue Violet, Titanium White, Napthol Crimson, Raw Umber, Sap Green Permanent, and Cadmium Yellow Light Hue
- 2" foam paintbrush
- #2 and #4 round paintbrushes
- General supplies: sandpaper, tracing paper, transfer paper, a palette, a container of water, paper towels, newspaper, and a toothbrush
- Wood glue
- Satin varnish

Paint It:

Rinse and blot the paintbrush on a paper towel between each color. Let the paint dry after each application. Use spray primer in a well-ventilated area.

1. Spray the tray and ball knobs with primer.
2. Use the 2" foam brush to paint the entire tray with two coats of Light Blue Violet. After the paint is dry, lightly sand the tray and wipe away the dust with a damp paper towel.
3. Trace, then transfer the pattern from page 29 onto the tray as shown.
4. Use the #4 round brush to paint the heart-shaped blossom petals with Titanium White.
5. Paint the heart-shaped strawberries with Napthol Crimson + Raw Umber.
6. Paint the leaves, stems, strawberry caps, and vines with Sap Green Permanent + Cadmium Yellow Light Hue.
7. Dot the blossom centers with Cadmium Yellow Light Hue.

8. Outline leaves and blossom centers as desired with Raw Umber.
9. Dot the strawberries and use the #2 round brush to paint the latticework along the edge of the tray with Titanium White.
10. Lightly sand the tray and wipe away the dust.
11. Spatter the tray with Raw Umber (see Dena's Tip for help spattering the tray).
12. Dot the ball knobs with Light Blue Violet and then glue them to the bottom of the tray for the "feet."
13. Apply two to three coats of varnish to the tray.

Dainty Duvet & Sham Set
Pages 23 & 24

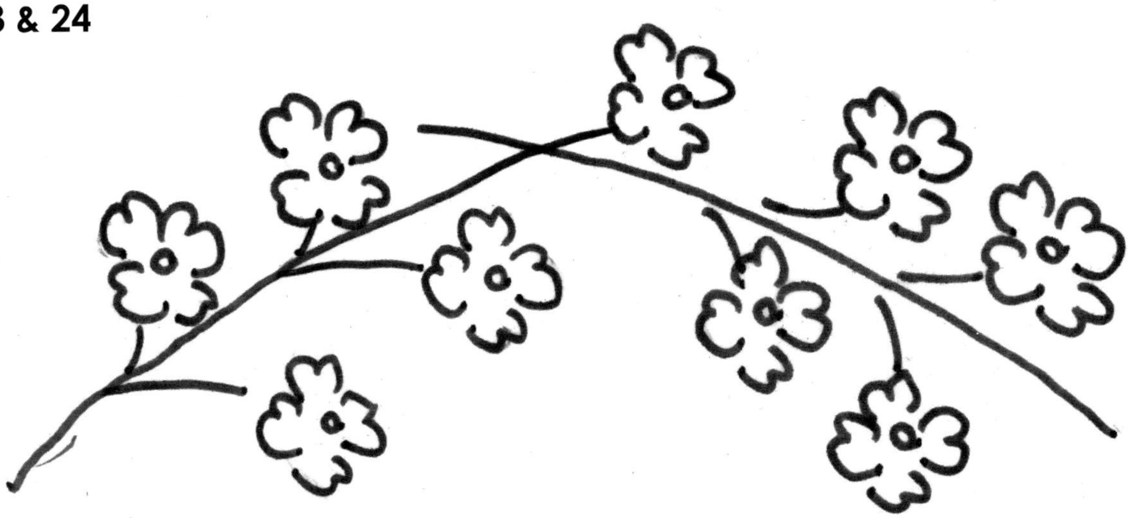

Petaled Placemat Set
Pages 17 & 18

Petaled Placemat Set
Pages 17 & 18

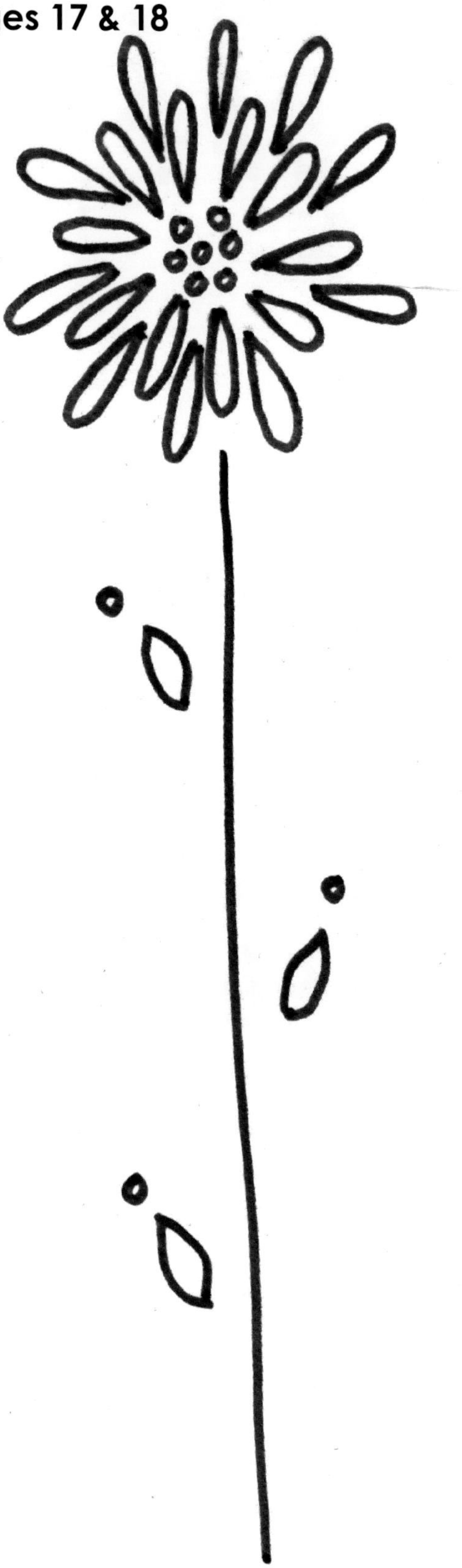

Berries & Blooms Tray
Pages 27 & 28

Appealing Pots
Pages 11 & 12

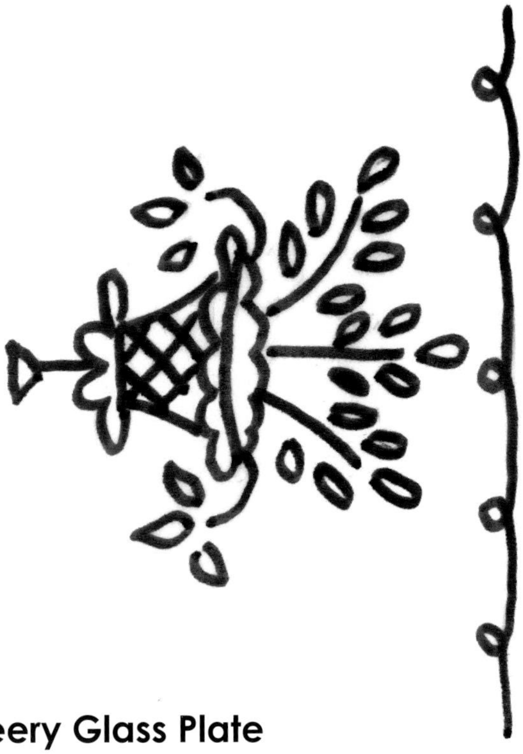

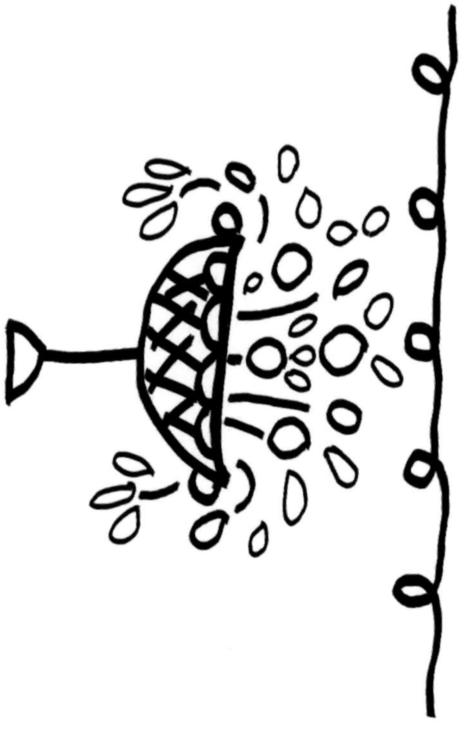

Cheery Glass Plate
Pages 13 & 14

My Notes

Sources

The surfaces and supplies needed to create the projects shown in this book should be readily available from local craft and fabric retailers, home décor and hardware stores, or online. Feel free to adjust and use the designs on alternative surfaces as necessary.

Production Team:

Technical Editor – Jennifer S. Hutchings

Senior Graphic Artist – Chaska Richardson Lucas

Production Artist – Stephanie Johnson

Photography Stylist – Cassie Francioni